101 LIFE QUOTES

Timeless Quotes to Change Your Life

HONEROD

ALSO BY HONEROD

The Daily Lesson

The NO-BS Self-Help Book

701 LIFE LESSONS

Visit www.honerod.com to follow Honerod and
stay up to date on future book releases

ISBN eBook: 979-8-89379-287-4

ISBN Paperback: 979-8-89379-285-0

ISBN Hardcover: 979-8-89379-283-6

 www.honerod.com

"A fine quotation is a diamond in the hand of a man of wit and a pebble in the hand of a fool. It is a good thing for an uneducated man to read books of quotations."

—

WINSTON CHURCHILL

POWER OF WORDS

"Words are, of course, the most powerful drug used by mankind."

— RUDYARD KIPLING

WORDS and quotes have the power to inspire, motivate, and challenge us in ways that can help us to grow and improve. They can offer us new perspectives and insights, and can help us to see things in a different light. Whether we are reading a book, listening to a speech, or having a conversation with a friend, the right words and quotes can have a profound impact on our thoughts and actions.

One of the reasons why quotes are so powerful is because they can capture the essence of an idea or thought in a concise and memorable way. A great quote can encapsulate a complex idea or emotion in just a few words, making it easier for us to understand and remember. This is why quotes are often used in speeches, writing, and other forms of communication — they can help to convey an idea in a way that is both powerful and memorable.

In addition to their ability to convey ideas in a concise and memorable way, quotes can also be used to stimulate the mind and unlock a more intimate connection with an audience. By carefully selecting and using quotes that resonate with you, I can create a deeper level of engagement and create a sense of shared understanding and connection. This is especially important when I'm trying to persuade or inspire you, as it helps to create a sense of common ground and build trust.

But quotes are not just useful for communicating with others — they can also be incredibly powerful for motivating and inspiring us. When we are faced with challenges or setbacks, a great quote can provide us with the encouragement and determination we need to keep going. They can remind us of our goals and the reasons why we are pursuing them and can give us the strength and confidence to overcome obstacles and achieve success.

Overall, words and quotes are invaluable tools for communication, inspiration, and motivation. Whether we are using them to challenge our own ideas, inspire and motivate others, or stimulate the mind, they have the power to change the way we think and act in profound ways.

101 Life Quotes is a book that stands out from the typical quote books you may see on the shelves. Rather than compiling a list of quotes from modern-day business leaders and motivational speakers, this book takes a different approach by featuring words and quotes from some of the greatest philosophers, authors, and exceptional people throughout history.

In a world that can often feel chaotic and overwhelming, the quotes in *101 Life Quotes* offer a moment of reflection and pause. They provide a chance to step back and consider the larger picture, and to think about the things that truly matter in life.

While this book may not contain quotes from well-known figures like Elon Musk, Jeff Bezos, or Tony Robbins, it is no less valuable or inspiring. In fact, the words and quotes featured in this book come from some of the greatest minds of all time and offer a wealth of wisdom and insight that can be applied to our lives today.

Enjoy your reading.

Twenty years from now you will be more disappointed by the things you didn't do than by the ones you did. So throw off the bowlines, sail away from the safe harbor. Catch the trade winds in your sails. Explore, Dream, Discover.

— **Mark Twain**

Too many people spend money they haven't earned... to buy things they don't want... to impress people they don't like.

— Will Rogers

The secret of happiness, you see is not found in seeking more, but in developing the capacity to enjoy less.

— **Socrates**

*Take care of your body. It's the
only place you have to live.*

— Jim Rohn

"

Every man has two lives, and the second starts when he realizes he has just one.

———

Confucius

In the middle of difficulty lies opportunity.

———

Albert Einstein

> **"**
>
> *Nobody can go back and start a new beginning, but anyone can start today and make a new ending.*
>
> —— Maria Robinson

Some people die at age 25 and aren't buried until they are 75.

— Benjamin Franklin —

"

Judge a man by his questions rather than his answers.

— Voltaire

When you find no solution to a problem, it's probably not a problem to be solved, but rather a truth to be accepted.

— **Proverb**

What is to give light must endure burning.

— Victor Frankl

"

Life isn't about finding yourself. Life is about creating yourself.

— George Bernard Shaw

> *To live is to suffer, to survive is to find some meaning in the suffering.*
>
> — Friedrich Nietzsche

Either you control the day or the day controls you.

— Honerod

"

More is lost by indecision than wrong decision.

— Marcus Tullius Cicero

If you don't create a plan for your life, someone will assign one to you.

Jim Rohn

"

The journey of a thousand miles begins with a single step.

— **Lao Tzu**

If there is no struggle, there is no progress.

— Frederick Douglas

"

Life can only be understood backwards; but it must be lived forwards.

———————

— **Søren Kierkegaard**

The tongue has no bones, but is strong enough to break a heart.

—— Proverb ——

We suffer more often in imagination than in reality.

— Seneca

To live is the rarest thing in the world. Most people exist, that is all.

— Oscar Wilde

If you are not willing to risk the unusual, you will have to settle for the ordinary.

——————

Jim Rohn

"

One day, in retrospect, the years of struggle will strike you as the most beautiful.

— Sigmund Freud

> **99**
>
> *Hard choices, easy life. Easy choices, hard life.*
>
> — Jerzy Gregorek

We are not rich by what we possess but by what we can do without.

— Immanuel Kant

> **99**
>
> *Nearly all men can stand adversity, but if you want to test a man's character, give him power.*
>
> — Abraham Lincoln

Luck is what happens when preparation meets opportunity.

— **Seneca**

Wealth consists not in having great possessions, but in having few wants.

— Epictetus

*Only when we can see through
ourselves can we see through others.*

—   Joseph Heller   —

We can't change the cards we are dealt, just how we play the hand.

Randy Pausch

"

*I'm a greater believer in luck, and
I find the harder I work the more I
have of it.*

— Thomas Jefferson

"

It is not death that a man should fear, but he should fear never beginning to live.

— **Marcus Aurelius**

If you change the way you look at things, the things you look at change.

Wayne Dyer

A healthy man wants a thousand things, a sick man only wants one.

— Confucius

"

Nothing is either good or bad, but thinking makes it so.

— William Shakespeare

The two most important days in your life are the day you're born and the day you find out why.

— Mark Twain

A gem cannot be polished without friction, nor a man perfected without trials.

———

Seneca

We have two ears and one mouth so that we can listen twice as much as we speak.

— Epictetus

"

If you hate a person, then you're defeated by them.

— Confucius

There is only one way to avoid criticism: do nothing, say nothing, and be nothing.

Aristotle

There is no illusion greater than fear.

— Lao Tzu

You can never cross the ocean until you have the courage to lose sight of the shore.

— Christopher Columbus

"

Care about what other people think and you will always be their prisoner.

— Lao Tzu

The future belongs to those who believe in the beauty of their dreams.

— Eleanor Roosevelt

"

It is during our darkest moments

that we must focus to see the light.

———————

Aristotle

99

Amateurs sit and wait for inspiration, the rest of us just get up and go to work.

— Stephen King

Failure is success in progress.

—   **Albert Einstein**   —

"

The only limit to our realization of tomorrow will be our doubts of today.

— Franklin D. Roosevelt

You are never too old to set another goal or to dream a new dream.

— C.S. Lewis

It takes 20 years to make an overnight success.

———

Eddie Cantor

Try not to become a person of success, but rather, try to become a person of value.

— Albert Einstein

The pessimist sees difficulty in every opportunity. The optimist sees opportunity in every difficulty.

— Winston Churchill

There are two different types of people in the world, those who want to know, and those who want to believe.

— Friedrich Nietzsche

Inspiration does exist, but it must find you working.

— Pablo Picasso

Gratitude is not only the greatest of virtues,

but the parent of all others.

— Cicero

66

I would rather die of passion than of boredom.

Vincent van Gogh

> *I was ashamed of myself when I realized that life was a costume party, and I attended with my real face.*
>
> — Franz Kafka

"

Fortune sides with him or her who dares.

— **Virgil**

I've learned that people will forget what you said, people will forget what you did, but people will never forget how you made them feel.

— Maya Angelou —

"

When one door of happiness closes, another opens, but often we look so long at the closed door that we do not see the one that has been opened for us.

— Helen Keller

A person who never made a mistake never tried anything new.

———

Albert Einstein

> **"**
> *The person who says it cannot be done should not interrupt the person who is doing it.*
>
> — Proverb

The greater the difficulty, the more the glory in surmounting it.

— Epicurus

A truly rich man is one whose children run into his arms when his hands are empty.

— Proverb

"

The fear of death follows from the fear of life. The man who lives fully is prepared to die at any time.

— Mark Twain

Remember that failure is an event, not a person.

Zig Ziglar

Don't live the same year 75 times
and call it a life.

Robin Sharma

66

Holding onto anger is like drinking poison and expecting the other person to die.

———————

Buddha

A comfort zone is a beautiful place, but nothing ever grows there.

— Honerod

It is never too late to be what you might have been.

— **George Eliot** —

He has the most who is most content with the least.

— Diogenes

Life is never made unbearable by circumstances, but only by lack of meaning and purpose.

— Victor Frankl

66

Instead of wondering when your next vacation is, maybe you should set up a life you don't need to escape from.

— Seth Godin

Don't let yesterday take up too much of today.

———

Will Rogers

"

A successful man is one who can lay a firm foundation with the bricks others have thrown at him.

— David Brinkley

Confidence is going after Moby Dick in a rowboat and taking the tartar sauce with you.

— Zig Ziglar

Small opportunities are often the beginning of great enterprises.

— Demosthenes

”

Build your own dreams, or someone else will hire you to build theirs.

— Farrah Gray

If you want your children to turn out well, spend twice as much time with them, and half as much money.

Abigail Van Buren

I have not failed. I've just found 10,000 ways that won't work.

Thomas Edison

"

Learn as if you will live forever, live

like you will die tomorrow.

———

Mahatma Gandhi

The best time to plant a tree was 20 years ago.
The second best time is now.

— **Chinese Proverb**

If you can't yet do great things,
do small things in a great way.

— Napoleon Hill —

"

Everything you've ever wanted is sitting on the other side of fear.

— George Addair

Success is walking from failure to failure with no loss of enthusiasm.

———

Winston Churchill

> *Don't be afraid to give up the good to go for the great.*
>
> — John D. Rockefeller

Life is either a daring adventure or nothing.

— Helen Keller

> **99**
>
> *We cannot solve problems with the kind of thinking we employed when we came up with them.*
>
> — Albert Einstein

In three words, I can sum up everything I've learned about life: it goes on.

— Robert Frost

The unexamined life is not worth living.

— **Socrates**

You only live once, but if you do it right, once is enough.

Mae West

Stay away from those people who try to disparage your ambitions. Small minds will always do that, but great minds will give you a feeling that you can become great too.

Mark Twain

"

The man who chases two rabbits,

catches neither.

———————

Confucius

If it won't matter in 5 years, don't spend more than 5 minutes getting angry about it.

— Honerod

Life is like riding a bicycle. To keep your balance, you must keep moving.

— Albert Einstein —

66

Ever tried. Ever failed. No matter. Try Again. Fail again. Fail better.

— Samuel Beckett

The single biggest problem in communication is the illusion that it has taken place.

George Bernard Shaw

"

He who has a why to live can bear almost any how.

— **Friedrich Nietzsche**

Unexpressed emotions will never die. They are buried alive and will come forth later in uglier ways.

— Sigmund Freud

> *It does not matter how slowly you go as long as you do not stop.*
>
> — Confucius

THANK YOU

T HANK you for taking the time to read my book. I hope that the quotes presented in these pages have been valuable to you and that they have inspired you to make positive changes in your life.

As an author, there is nothing more rewarding than knowing that my work has positively impacted someone's life. Whether you were looking to improve your health, mindset, relationships, or career, I hope this book has provided you with the guidance and inspiration you needed to move forward.

In light of this, I kindly ask for a moment more of your time to leave a review of the book through the link provided below. Your review greatly assists in broadening the book's visibility, enabling it to reach and resonate with a larger audience.

 https://www.honerod.com

 phonerodb@gmail.com

www.ingramcontent.com/pod-product-compliance
Lightning Source LLC
Chambersburg PA
CBHW061433160726
47995CB00003B/879